WOLF
AND
PILOT

Also by Farrah Field

Rising

Wolf
and
Pilot

Farrah Field

Megan! Sorry to miss you at Tom's wedding, but so good to read w/ you @ Diane Tapes!

Four Way Books
Tribeca

Please direct all inquiries to:
Editorial Office
Four Way Books
POB 535, Village Station
New York, NY 10014
www.fourwaybooks.com

Library of Congress Cataloging-in-Publication Data

Field, Farrah.
  [Poems. Selections]
  Wolf and pilot / Farrah Field.
     pages cm
  ISBN 978-1-884800-99-3 (pbk.)
  I. Title.
  PS3606.I33W65 2012
  811'.6--dc23

                              2012002006

This book is manufactured in the United States of America
and printed on acid-free paper.

Four Way Books is a not-for-profit literary press. We are grateful for the assistance
we receive from individual donors, public arts agencies, and private foundations.

This publication is made possible with public funds
from the National Endowment for the Arts

and from the New York State Council on the Arts, a state agency.

This book was supported in part by a Face Out grant
from the Council of Literary Magazines and Presses, funded by
the New York Community Trust.

[clmp]   We are a proud member
           of the Council of Literary Magazines and Presses.

Distributed by University Press of New England
One Court Street, Lebanon, NH 03766

For My Husband,
Jared White

CONTENTS

The Smartest Person in the Room Never Speaks 3
We Left Before My Turn 4
The Girls Bury Themselves for Two Weeks 6
The Girls Gather Around While He Sleeps 7
Not All Henrys Are Hucks or Hanks 8
Mother's Children Don't Come When She Calls 9
The Girls Approach the Fence 10
Desperate Mothers Are Easy Lays 12
Elsianne Celebrates Her Birthday 14

Bedtime Stories 19
Wanting to Train Pigmy Goats 20
Emaline Develops an Attachment 22
Maybe You Have More Than One Private Parts 24
The Teacher Explains Urgency to the Detective 26
The Detective Wonders If He Said Something Wrong 27
Den 28
Bomber Jacket 29
The Girls Talk of Troilus 30
Our Food Will Not Come from a Cigarette Company 31

Are You a Wild Animal or a Baby 35
Aubrie Steals the Key To 36
Mother Talks to Herself Before Hunting Her Children 37
Tall People Have Hurt Knees 38
The Detective Is Dismissed 40
Human Hair Paintbrush 41

The Girls Give Helen the Checking Account   42
Blood Is Best When a Woman Is in Trouble   43
Red Onion Paper   44
The Witch Stands Beyond the Vapor   45
Matilda Stays Up Late With No Questions to Ask   46

Elsianne Walks Between Quiet Rooms   49
Dark Thirty Will Come Early   50
How to Build the Family Robot   51
Lines of Varying Heaviness   52
Emaline's Afterlife Self Remembers Her Detective Crush   54
Elsianne Heads Off to a Bright Future   55
Dalebound   56

Notes

We don't know how the sisters crawled out of the window,
the detective said, counting footsteps from the rocking chair
to the window, from the desk to the window as if the girls,
scattered around the room, one by one got up and left.

Lincoln and his son hang above the fireplace hardware.
The girls called him "the fifth." They thought they would
catch tuberculosis from the portrait. There were Revolutionary
soldiers in the family. The girls wanted to register their names.

Child-size chairs made the detective feel tall in an old way.
He stood in the bay near the Gothic Revival windows.
The four sisters were like deer taking a rose
without any sign they had been there or would return.

Unfinished wooden boxes were stacked on the floor.
Their teacher said the girls worked together, scoring
one notch at a time. Planning how all sisters plan.
They reupholstered a parlor chair with dark green denim.

No one knows how big houses came to exist, how anyone
could walk in on a daily basis, mount a war-period wall clock,
pollute the cold kitchen with pork dumplings, heat the toilet seat.
The detective wondered if the girls knew how to ride bicycles.

Four wool coats were gone. There was no way to console
the cross-armed mother, who made the detective nervous,
even after she went down to her kitchen, peered over
the Dutch door and sure enough, a porcelain leg.

We Left Before My Turn

We placed the leg outside the door and the rest
twenty miles in the wrong direction. Old doll,
false lead. Running away is easy

when you hardly talk to your mother.
She ate snails once. But did you see her chew them?
I've never seen her chew anything.

We didn't speak until a week underground.
No one was stitchy. We measured time
by plastic cereal bowls. Our mother appeared

in the garden once. She ran a long nail
up my spine. You should keep a back like that
covered, she said. I'm the littlest. I asked her

what she was doing there. She had powder
on her face; I could see it in the hairs.
She said she'd been up for eight days.

I didn't look in her eyes as she walked
circles around me. She said I'd never guess
what she was going to do with the turtle

wiggling in her hands, gasping for breath.
It was beyond shrinking into its shell, flaying
the air as though it could swim home.

That is the only time I ate dinner with her.
My orange suitcase smells like my duck.
Our mother probably smashed the eggs

by now. I wonder why she never arranged
babysitters for us. Because you had me, Matilda says.
She's returned from the surface. It's May.

The Girls Bury Themselves for Two Weeks

We think the worst thing a parent can do is love one child less than the others. When the sun comes out, we'll walk twenty pounds less in cut sleeves. We'll burn so badly we'll think skinny wildfire and kiss each other all over the arms. While we are away from the world we are wise and sound wise. If we were rabbits we'd be shot dead and hanging in a pantry by now. Tell us, are we runaways if we walked out of the heavy front door? Unlocked and footfall. The ground sticks to our mother's lipgloss and she doesn't like anything except maybe cat hair sticking to her chanthole. We've never had Winesap apples before, never blue potatoes. We don't even know snow, winter, mugs. How do we know what these things are? Down here we still hear noises. We won't live in this hole much longer.

THE GIRLS GATHER AROUND WHILE HE SLEEPS

You're not as smart as you'd like to be, but you're smarter than you think.
The day has been long and you've accomplished less.
The crab-mauling scar on your foot hangs over the bed.
We picture you growing up on a shore.
Once a group moves another group is changed.
We pushed the Bighorns further out
and we didn't mean to do that.
Living near people is like living inside.
You smell like our teacher.
She wrapped strawberry preserves and Brazilian nuts
in brown paper. You left them in your locked car.
The note we wrote hangs above the nearby desk.
Helen Gale. 3691 Coffee Avenue.
You think you might be on to something.
Your arms are crossed as though you fell asleep thinking.
We wonder if you'll sleep so soundly next to her,
if she'll make pumpkin pancakes.
It's easy to know when someone's in your house:
listen for a tack being pulled from the wall and paper falling.
When you look for people smarter than you, you look for them.
There are four of us and when we move, eight steps are taken.
We can go no further than your pastures
because we arrived without a trace and no one can do that again
unless by vanishing. A mountain lion hunts your land.
She doesn't frighten us. She says no one chooses her own mother
but she's wrong. We weren't born like other people.
Helen will brew tea for you later. Something has to happen.

The detective studies bites. One of the girls
lost an eyetooth in a fig by his house.
There were no secret instructions among their things.
The girls can talk just by thinking.
While watching television, Henry reminds himself
that the dancing butt in short shorts
and a yellow belt is someone's daughter.
The four girls belong to themselves.
A daughter isn't one for long.
After a month, Henry sat in the park
with milk and warm cookies.
Women warned him to protect his suit from mulberries.
A boy Henry found years ago passed by.
The girls wished he knew they weren't going home.
One cookie had cranberries and chocolate.
It was their favorite.
He wondered what they did for food.
The mother never fed them.
They watched him from lawn chairs
behind the summer jazz band.
Using craft scissors and felt
they constructed this very scene.
This is how the detective cooks:
he opens a drawer
and everything falls out.
He always found his kids.
They admired his plate,
how he didn't let anyone else have any.
They were never offered cookies before.

Here, Elsianne. You knitted yourself into a sewing machine. Stir and wash for the girls. Love like a school and teach them not to lie. Sister activities: movies, kitty beauty salon, hating your mother. You threw tomatoes on the hay bales. Fishbones and spray paint, a collage. Your sisters listen to you.

Here, Matilda. You smell like a nap. One day you will have the middle to yourself. Are you a hard wooden saddle, whoever thought of that. Do you have a car. Will you pick me up and take me. Aren't middle children amicable. You're smart, bumble-headed. You left the keys near a bull.

My Emaline. One M not two. You snuck down the stairs while the others slept. Guess what's under this cloth. You will won't you, one little life. Sticker for postcard. I watched your calves move under your skin when you reached for the door on tippy toes. I tickled what grew on the bottom of your foot, an X.

Here, Aubrie. The youngest is ageless. I never counted. One of the girls, lowering the average height. Take the detective's thumb. You're a generation away from dying. President, comic book club. You lie when you say you have no recollection of me. Did you really think I needed that knife you took.

THE GIRLS APPROACH THE FENCE

Detective, we think you're afraid of spiders. You'd be surprised
to know what things are in your shed. We think you should feed us.

No one will ever know. Preserves, beets—anything you don't want.
We'll put the crumbs in our pockets. We'll drink lime soda.

We won't tell anyone your middle name, that your ancestors
fired at pilots, that you donate funds to help build

a bridge. We like apple butter. Your house is so brickly
and your stove so cold and lonesome for bread.

We've been eating your flowers. We'll stop if you want us to.
Whatever you throw out, we'll eat like raccoons. The tall one

is a ballerina. Our mother never took pictures of us.
We fixed the shed's leaks. Before, we had to sit on sawhorses

and watch water run under the walls then downhill.
You must've had a grandfather pass. We miss our lessons.

One of your dogs has a deer tick. At least give us one sheep.
Flash four lights when you want us. We'll give you pieces

of information. Our mother breast-fed far too long.
We want our tongues blue with lollipops.

The little one thinks she would like bubble gum ice cream.
We practice talking to you. We think you know that.

Our teacher taught everything—boxing lessons, robotics.
This is what they sell at flea markets, she said.

Aubrie imagines what it'd be like to walk on carpet, to have a roll of candy
to save for later. Shh. You weren't supposed to say my name.

Desperate Mothers Are Easy Lays

All they remember of him is their returned children.
Speak with bait or don't speak. It's easy to use someone's body.

During the time of hysteria, women were brought down manually.

The detective plus someone could bring a case to a guessing point.
Both people are thoughtful because they want justice.

Sluts and prostitutes—they're funny words to say, as if
they were the same, as if knowing a few were knowing the whole.

The mothers were like pulling a hangnail and watching the blood
rush back and forth underneath until it pops up to drown the tear.

Who could possibly know what someone else looks like anyway.

A habit of bodies is like lighting a stick on fire and breathing.
Under our fresh outfits, we're variations of wolves at best.

Someone isn't greeting him with tears, won't allow him inside.
He doesn't regard her as a mother of four girls.

They visit his house, decorate his desk with chalk drawings,
leak their teacher's number on receipt backs.

Prints on a wooden spoon. The girls must've cooked.

He called their everyone loves teachers.
Something tells him he is about to have a family.

Who's running this case here? The detective never can tell.

ELSIANNE CELEBRATES HER BIRTHDAY

I want a candle in a cupcake
given to me in a hollow tree.

This year aging matters.
Last year I spoke to rabbits.

One hundred years ago this day
a miner was covered up to his neck.

The weasel that chewed his face
offered a kind of company.

My sisters crafted tiny cards for me.
I found one underneath my big toe.

Mother didn't know we knew
our birthdays. Twelve children died

of polio on mine. Fourteen of fifteen
September birthday holders

learn to be overlooked.
Here and there without a coat still.

I never went to school.
From our room,

I watched the rusted-clutch bus
choke its way to select houses.

It's lonely being the oldest.
Maybe someone will invent medication

made without wild duck hearts.
I give myself up to this world of freedom.

Remember when our mother told us we had small pox.
We are one two three four girls who have no father
because our mother is the father is a witch. We were
in bed and a kettle whistled for a very long time.

One day a girl named Abigail rang the house bell.
We were sweating we were homing. The witch
put on skin with moles and asked yes with her eyebrows.
Abigail pointed. This is no castle to put barefoot feet on

but Elsianne stood up anyway. We were never sick
or in the woods. A clitoris could be pinned down
like a dissected frog the witch said. Abigail said
what are you talking about and went away the only

friend we ever had. We are stronger than blackbirds
we don't know what anything means we put our
hands on the cool glass called a window.
Once upon a time all adults used to be children.

Wanting to Train Pigmy Goats

Aubrie makes the sign of sleep
and points to dead animals.
On one side, they're comfy and curled
yet smashed on the other.

We'll never say this: we want to hang
a sheet from a tree and project movies.
Hail pings as though the air were water
and the water a cranberry bog.

We think being sad is better than being dead.
Our mother can pull her face off at the nostril.
We don't build fires. We sit in wet grass
and whisper our teacher's name.

Old service roads have old houses.
No fences means no dogs.
We know where sheep slept.
We use leaves to push away the poop.

While we hide in trees, a horse family
stands close together in a big field—
we are cold too—and a man pushes
a long hose on wheels in the other field.

Our mother makes nightmares for us
with a lamp and a bunny.
She says you can electrocute someone
from any place on the body.

She threw one of her feet at us and never lost her balance.

Emaline Develops an Attachment

You always turn a street too soon by my mother's house.

This is what it's like to be bored in summer,
to sit cross-legged and wish you hadn't
in the heavy air with no approaching future

except kiwi. The older sisters mimic
swim strokes until they sweat under their arms.
We kept your gun in its holster for two days.

I wonder what you're like when you're cold.

Six times we've caught you talking to yourself.
We want to present you with a ball rolled from twigs.
We saw you at the county records office.

I can't help whom I think about the most.

Have you ever been to Chicago
or washed a glass with the fog of your breath?
Soon it will be time to mail the letter.

You sing the same song in the shower.
Every Sunday, you throw an empty bottle
at St. Rita's services sign.

If it rains, the cigarette behind your ear
will turn into splinters and mush.
We know you don't do you know I wrapped

grass around my fingers and married you.

Maybe You Have More Than One Private Parts

Thank you for waking us up and freaking us out,

for turning on all the lights after we fell asleep.
We hid under the dining room chairs.

We cried when you plugged that thing into the wall.

No more loud music, we said,
no more people who stare and don't talk.

Helen entered through the back door
where a chipmunk scampered.
You tied our hands together

and straightened a hanger.

Thank you for choosing our birth order.
We know what took place on the lower levels.

It lasted for a long time,
with you and others in the middle,
spilling your drinks in each other.

Then hands all over before one at the face and one below.

The people you brought crowded around.
There could never be too many

ready to act on your fake body.
They stood with their legs apart

waiting for you to choose them.
Helen sat with us in our room
when things were getting started.

Leaves collected on the ceiling panel.
We painted deer nibbling bugs on their hindquarters.

By morning, most of the people were hooded.

At the same time every day,
we all heard the crop duster fly over.

An unknown force is always.
We think we function
under a kind of freedom.
Dirt could be in your house.
Never underestimate what pulses.
Two men watching.
Reaching underneath camisoles.
Girls are prey to everything.
They're only daughters for a little while.
They think kindness could spare their lives.
Their tiny lives, tiny as wrists.
Don't stay in a house without electricity.
Never walk around during dreams
and never throw a piece of paper
on the ground. Suck blood
from a cut finger
before someone else does.
If a fish were to flop your way,
look up. Kidnapper downpour.
Finger in a mouth and skirt in a tree.
Don't roll around on big leaves.
The earth is seed.
Beware of taking off your shirt.
The rye will tickle your nipples.

THE DETECTIVE WONDERS IF HE SAID SOMETHING WRONG

No one says you're over-worked—
certainly not booted-tired and early,
              never job-pissy.

You never say, were you sleeping the whole time,
              don't eat those,
        or you expect me to find where we are on the map?

How'd you know about the Harbor Master's house,
city-shadowed in a world of garbage bags full of leaves.

Maybe love wonders what the world is—
              shouldn't this, tortured that—

and how to buy a house and have babies.

                    Or love could be dandruff—
an excuse for one to say oy at the other's collar.

I bet you get headaches
              thinking so much.
              You're the smartest person I know.

                    Somewhere a big dog barks gong-like.
        I wish it ran to me, putting its ears down,
              mine when I called,
and we walked together without a leash or choke chain.

DEN

Do you want to go down like that, soapy and sleepy.
Lip balm is soft as flesh is soft beneath all that wool

and whatever else. You have a ferocious outline standing up.
May I pull a line of floss for you? No one needs a ticket

for a show here, windows, the projector, striped sheets
in the laundry pile, something floating in the bathwater,

a fan. I'll erect you in bronze, melt you in a spontaneous
temple fire then erect you again. What do I look like

when you touch me. Is my mouth wide enough for tonsils.
We slide to the floor until those jeans are folded

over the ladder, listening to albums, two swallows of rum
and tomato juice in the morning. Watering pots of cilantro.

For lunch you roll burritos on heated plates.
Inside there are nutrients, possibilities, safety.

BOMBER JACKET

Elsianne picks her own fabric and her own patterns,
but the others like what I sew for them.
Eggs for breakfast she says and I say sure.
She says this radish sprout and mushroom salad
should be served in the wooden bowl.
I believe every word. The salad had mint.
Emaline still hasn't changed her clothes.
Matilda says she wants to blue in the ocean.
I wanted to joke that I could borrow
their mother's broomstick, but Elsianne walks in,
demands a calendar. Soap cures around the house
and Aubrie asks when we can use it in the claw bath.
Everyone holds her. Guess who told Henry to get a job
he's good at and guess who bales hay down the street.
Friday nights they're allowed to sleep anywhere they choose.

Consider the possibility.

Everyone likes poop.

The weight of his armor equaled three of us.

We learn how to love during lessons.

We want someone who can handle us.

We sit on the wall and watch him pass.

From the book with the war and a woman.

What are you supposed to do besides what you have to?

He loves older women. They were lovers through the gapped stones.

Our parents have that look again.

Replacement. Kneecap eyes. Dress with only a center.

We have everything to look forward to when we grow up.

We never dip quick bread in our stone house.
We peel tomatoes. We poke them with cloves.
It's all local because there isn't anywhere else.

Organic hand cream, even pistachios.
We can do anything if we take a class.

The detective's pantry has never been
so fully full, enough for disaster.
Food brands for children sound gross.

Our teacher needs a potato masher and time to think,
watching us hold the seeds, bored to sticks.

We can never be too aware of what's really being said.
The detective sweated with the shovel
that kept hitting a large stone. He threw

his heavy coat on a pile of dirt. His own air
circled his face and the teacher told him not to swear.

When he fell down, we took the shovel,
Elsianne at the handle, the two little ones
jumped on the blade. We're strong

as blueberries. Matilda stood between the adults,
saying we shall call them parents.

What are you girls doing, lined up on the floor like that.
We change our teacher's pillowcase. Will she lean toward us

using her better ear in the daylight? Our cat sits on the edge
of the bedpost. He blinks when we talk to him. We wish

she'd let us wash her, the bloodstain near her shoulder.
She says lemon ought to work, but she doesn't have

her balance yet maybe she never will. Her face doesn't
go sour when she cries. Tears roll into the moonlight

as though someone left the faucet on. She twists
and squirms beneath the bedclothes and brings out

the blue nightgown in a bundle. It is perfectly
see-through and we wonder which one of us will

take it from her. We are all looking at her bare arm extended,
her hand holding the sheet to cover her boobies.

We crawl onto the bed. We think her ear looks like a fetus.
Exploding Velcro is all she hears in one ear. It's too soon

to wipe the dried blood. She says it hurts like hell. We hurt
like hell too and our detective isn't home yet.

Tomorrow we will make cedar boxes. We have
a long time to get used to this new loud ringing.

I heard you love falling.
How come dress up the detective doesn't?
It's a party! It's a date! It's a party!
Stand on a chair with paper napkins.
Music from a button.
Have your peat and eat it too.
Ponytails? I have board games.
Smart children are very expressive.
Being afraid is very expensive.
Old everyone around here.
Naked bodies show comic books.
Hands never talked before.
They say the youngest is most.
I spilled sticky on the tablecloth.
The TV only works for the detective.
Hammer don't. *She's just acting out.*
Who here has sexy parents.

MOTHER TALKS TO HERSELF BEFORE HUNTING HER CHILDREN

There's no need to investigate kindness. You were
never a *there, there* back patter. You melted their

coloring sticks to the carpet and they trailed radishes
that ended at a pile of fortified bobcat poop.

They knew you were a witch before you told them.
For the firstborn, you wished her never to suffer illness.

Then you wanted all of them sick with fever so you could
wipe their sweaty arms below the blankets. The oldest

cared for them and you watched her from your mind,
wringing a cloth in cold water, resting to knit more cloths,

humming tunes you never taught her. You laughed
when you saw their little panties hung on the laundry line,

wind bobbing elastic legs-holes like a xylophone.
Everyone who thinks babies solve loneliness is wrong.

You washed your face with menstrual blood
until they caught you. When they ran away, you realized

they were what you wanted all along. You had perfect people,
but you were biting the heads off, well, it doesn't matter.

Your daughters never needed you even when you forced them.

Tall People Have Hurt Knees

Helen asked if I thought she was wearing underwear

She kept her lips

There was a drop of piss but I didn't care

By my hand she pulled me to the ground

She is very flexible she said tell me what you've never told anyone

We snuck to the bathroom when the girls were asleep

I can fix anything even my own knee

Which fog is it

I hadn't noticed her height until she turned around and gripped the sink

We didn't want the girls to hear us

I can come just by looking at you

Some hair stuck to her bottom lip her breath fogged the mirror

The Mother pulls a brick from the wall

She followed me home when I lost my job

When you have something a witch wants

It's still a wall no crumbling just one brick missing

Hit hard enough the leg will bend in a weird direction

My kneecap is a floating broken shield and the tendons are desperate

She barely moves her hand like whisking

She says the man is hurt and I will take one of my girls

I say did you really think I protected them

You can't ask someone who can not to kill you

Helen comes through the snow and carries me home

Love is in love with me

You're wearing those hose they were hanging in the bathroom

She puts a log on the fire

I can make you get so wet

The girls bring her a towel and a bucket of ice for my knee

THE DETECTIVE IS DISMISSED

The order was top-heavy, paperworky, cigar smokey.
Our detective said he was informed before the end

of the work day. We wanted to walk home with him.
We wanted to be hunchy shoulders with him.

I'll show them where the teacher spends her nights, he said.
He wasn't a very good detective when we think about it.

His hats were not hats before dinner. Our mother
visited the Lieutenant. She multiplied herself, licked

both of his waxy ears, and straddled both of his legs.
One of her walked on his desk and didn't get up there

by jumping! She kicked the paperclips around and pressed
one of her bare feet on his chest, stuck a toe in his mouth.

The other one of her did something else. You didn't tell
them the girls live with us did you, our teacher asked.

We are the girls. Everything in the world points to us,
not in a girls-will-be-girls kind of way.

Human Hair Paintbrush

This is what I used to do for cash.

If we're a family, we've got to have money.

Henry recovers on the settee.

He wonders if he should tell the girls
not to put their elbows on the table.

You think I'd know what to do
because I agreed to take care of them.

Aubrie had bangs
and Emaline, creek-shine.

Matilda says she'll will her stubbles red.

Henry looks for the familiar when we get home.
I told him to finish knitting the girls' socks.

There are burdens to go all around.

The Girls Give Helen the Checking Account

Helen says the detective is the male version of Loretta Lynn.

She bought him malt liquor with the change

he was saving for a new shirt. The man can't garden for shit

and she doesn't know how ends are supposed to meet.

Helen's lip quivers as she pours milk into equal parts in clear glasses.

Suddenly she gasps and shoves her hand into the flour colander

and throws a handful that powders the dishes piled in the sink.

I have to take care of cock 'n balls and these girls? She cries

and her hair seems browner and longer every time she cries.

Elsianne pets Helen's arms and tells her about a mining town

covered with the white dust of minerals that preserve wet cakes.

Let us worry, we say. You should roast the zucchini

and fill the house with your kind banner that you painted

on old newspaper. Let us pay for the burden of us. Lettuce,

Aubrie says. Matilda giggles. We giggle. Helen giggles.

BLOOD IS BEST WHEN A WOMAN IS IN TROUBLE

When you sleep, your mumbles smell breathy.
You can hum while you eat a sandwich.
The girls said cats have two voice boxes.
What is the worst thing you ever did to someone you love?
You said you didn't like how the market
handled their lobsters, the assembly line of it all.
What is corrupt has to have something to corrupt.
Sometimes I catch you perfectly balanced on the banister.
Why would you sit up there? What about your dress?
I ordered the wrong-sized bag. An emotion is about
to be revealed in the pond. My phone is still in my pocket
while you hold me for ten seconds underwater.
You said it's better to swim with your clothes on
because it makes you truly weightless.

RED ONION PAPER

See the crocodile noses as they sleep in the water.
Whoever thought a body could hang like that.
Suspended in the pond, bottomless brown.
When we swim, we'll roll our hair around our faces one hundred times.
A pair of claws works as good as hands.
The crocodiles will assume we're already caught.
They won't trust the commotion.
We avoid being eaten by pretending the thing has already eaten.
There could be a bus-sized catfish down there.
Our mother drinks the debris in a mug.
Our mother waits behind a log.
With her hair caught on the reeds and her mouth open.

The Witch Stands Beyond the Vapor

It's only a pile of sticks in the woods.
My sisters go to bed after me.
It's only a pile of sticks

arranged counter-clockwise, like a funnel.

A long time from now,
my sisters will say I wanted to die.

Mother plans something she shouldn't.

Our teacher is scared of someone waiting
where she can't see, someone really there,
mouthing words I can't hear,

not slipping in the spot I slip in.
Someone's always watching,

but never where you think.

My sisters don't know
I'm really clear-headed.
When my mother twitches outside the window,

I know what she wants me to do.
It's only a pile of sticks like I'm a pile of sticks.

Matilda Stays Up Late With No Questions to Ask

Even a week later
        Emaline's hand is clear
    sitting in the leaves like soap in a bowl.

It's easy to discern when a body is dead.
                Most of us are animals.
        Most of us know when we're not alone.

A head that doesn't turn toward on-leaf footsteps isn't alive.

You don't have to touch it to know.
                Even when we saw the blood in the yard.
        The holes all over her body came next.

All you had to do was look at her hand.
                If you weren't thinking about your sister.
        If you weren't huffing the cold air.

Elsianne Walks Between Quiet Rooms

This is not a dream kind of dream.

Spanish moss has taken us over,

gone down the jawlines,

around the necks,

and pokes from our sleeves.

Not even the chairs creak anymore.

Walking around a grieving household

makes you think it could be picked up

in the palm and put in the oven.

Come on, little house. Say something.

Father, Mother, Sister, Sister, Sister, Dead Sister.

DARK THIRTY WILL COME EARLY

You could hear the family if you were sitting on the roof
The pizza-making carrot-picking and beads to sell
Who cries the loudest and who comforts the softest
All those years spent figuring out
How to be above genus and craft
And see who'd take after the adopted mother
Who'd liken the adopted father who'll never
Be the same accidentally setting the table
For six now five they were used to saying six
They had four children they have three
As soon as someone hands you a bucket of hope
Someone else hands you a tray full of shards
Saying lift this can't you lift this is this too heavy
The real mother knew the entire time
Where her little things were how happy they were
She gnawed her teeth until they crumbled
The voices of one thousand evil trumpets filled her
She took off her underwear and rubbed the chimney
No one should ever like torture

Find an old bike with the mind still in it.
Put little screws into your sewed-on pockets.
The youngest has skinny arms
that will place parts further into the engine.
Where is the new planet in relation to the old planets?
The second oldest is one middle of two middles.
She installs the heat exchanger.
How will we get to where we're going
and is the small freezer filled with mochi ice cream?
Transition is like metal and metal fuses by heavy ion science.
People with absent mothers are better at self-preservation.
Anything can be done while thinking about a dead sister.
As the oldest, I often experience frustration before awe.

They said winter was approaching.
Clouds unraveled, passed over,
leaving shadow-patches
like liver spots on buildings and children.
Sometimes days rained for no purpose.
There was nothing to water,
no chance of sleet or fog,
and fountains were shut off
at the supposed end of summer.
A pack of polar bears drowned
for lack of ice floe
off the coast of Greenland.
Hats and mittens await.
Someone shook his head
regarding a melted ski resort.
Thank heavens a scarf is always in style.
Time isn't controlled very well—
a rotation took three seconds longer.
Future years are off a bit.
Winter may never happen again.
Wolf protested,
eating only flowers
and her babies.
Someone said it was apocalyptical
and hid a sunflower in a blue box
with a white moth.
Sun-streaked hair remains
and there is no snow
collecting on a marquee

about to collapse.
Nor is it being watched
by the caretaker who knows
if it were cold outside,
he'd be on the ladder
wearing water resistant gloves,
snow crawling up his sleeve.

Emaline's Afterlife Self Remembers Her Detective Crush

I imagine we're so old that we don't care what play we attend.
You refrain from asking me to repeat what I've said.
I wear a Burberry coat that I haven't taken off. As the curtain
rises, I'm flooded with light, asleep within minutes.
Your head bobs as though someone were scratching your back
and touched a sensitive spot every few seconds. I dream about
the first time I saw you—tired, bags under your eyes like small plums.
When my sisters visited, you looked at them with awe—
the only ones who knew about our mother the witch.
When I finally relaxed, you were there in a frame
and sitting under a quilt. We laughed over tea. You insisted
I dye my hair and after ten years, reveal my name.
I wake up to applause and ask if you have to use the toilet.
You say no, but tell me that you've loved me for a long, long time,
more than my sisters, that you knew I was a survivor
the moment you caught me following you in the woods.

ELSIANNE HEADS OFF TO A BRIGHT FUTURE

Parents think they are the only ones who suffer.

I didn't bring anything with me to college except everything in the car.

This new town isn't meatless.
There's only one way to know if a man is beautiful.

Whoever thought you'd have to go away to become smarter.
It's all so gradual yet sudden because everyone is crying.

I'd like to take back something I said when I was young.

Women on campus don't like my dorm room.
The lights are never on.
My sisters crawl out from under the bed.

Then our parents suffered more because
they realized they couldn't suffer like us.

My sisters said I should be a doctor.

How am I going to get through the next year? They said, watch this.

DALEBOUND

We open the grassy door
of the future. Our eventually
dead mother jack-in-the-box

pops out and says, *This is just
like heaven! This is just like
heaven!* One of us hums,

sweeps the woolen floor.
In this room we learn
what people really thought

about us, the result of all
those pizza dinners, time with
Nicole, Eli, Boogie, where

a nest was,
and how the space
our sister took was never

reoccupied. In the future
we are further along
without her, lick one

of the other's nostrils,
then tie a leather string
for orange bracelets.

We sit on woven chairs
inside, think our own
time better for its sameness,

and right when we think
there was a past meant for all
four of us, with feathers

and less junk, the little
future is gone and we'll
never remember what

we briefly saw. We'll crave
tall drinks that taste
like the future, we'll want

on our laps its softness,
a linen box that holds bowls
of warm ropey noodles.

NOTES

Details in "The Smartest Person in the Room Never Speaks"
are based on arrangements of Narcissa Thorne's miniature diorama,
"Middletown Parlor," which measures 10 1/8 x 21 x 18 1/2 inches.

Tensions in "The Teacher Explains Urgency to the Detective" are inspired
by the film *Picnic at Hanging Rock*, directed by Peter Weir.

The crop duster in "Maybe You Have More Than One Private Parts"
refers to a plane heard flying overhead by a test subject undergoing long-
term sensory deprivation during a series of mind control experiments
led by Ewen Cameron and funded by the CIA. The plane flew over at 9
a.m. every morning, connecting the subject to the outside world, despite
Cameron's attempts to dismantle his patient's sense of space and time.
Cameron's experiments began in the early 1950's and ended in 1961. Naomi
Klein discusses them in her book, *The Shock Doctrine: The Rise of Disaster
Capitalism*.

"Blood Is Best When a Woman Is in Trouble" is a refraction of the phrase
"A brave man's blood is the best thing when a woman is in trouble," from
Dracula by Bram Stoker.

"Lines of Varying Heaviness" is taken from the writings of Paul Klee.

The word "dalebound" first appears in the poem "Fauning" by Ross Brighton.

ACKNOWLEDGMENTS

Heartfelt gratitude to the editors of the following publications, where poems from *Wolf and Pilot* first appeared, some in different form and title:

42Opus, Cannibal, Copper Nickel, Ekleksographia, Harp & Altar, La Petite Zine, Linebreak, LUNGFULL! Magazine, Mantis, The Pinch, Ploughshares, The Raleigh Quarterly, and *Typo.*

"The Girls Talk of Troilus" appears at the end of "We Will Learn to Feel Quite Clean in This New Skin," an essay for *Coldfront's* Poets Off Poetry series.

Linebreak published, along with the poem, a recording of "Matilda Stays Up Late With No Questions" read by Brad Leithauser.

Several poems from this book have been translated into Serbian and appear in the anthology, *The Day Lady Gaga Died: An Anthology of Contemporary New York Poetry,* edited by Ana Božičević and Željko Mitić.

Complementary poems featuring characters from *Wolf and Pilot* are collected in the chapbook *Parents,* published by Immaculate Disciples Press in 2011. One poem from *Parents* appears in *Wolf and Pilot.*

I am grateful for the continual support of Four Way Books, especially Martha Rhodes and Ryan Murphy. Thank you for awarding me time at the Fine Arts Work Center in Provincetown, Massachusetts.

Thank you Dan Magers, Steven Karl, Richard Scheiwe, Kaveh Bassiri, Lauren Ireland, Molly Dorozenski, Steve Roberts, Ian Dreiblatt, Aubrie Marrin, Julia Cohen, Paige Taggart, Sampson Starkweather, Cynthia Arrieu-King, Matthew and Katy Henriksen, and Keith Newton for your friendship and invaluable editorial feedback. For my family, Field and White, I can't thank you enough for your love and encouragement. Jared White, I love you I love you I love you I love you.

Farrah Field is the author of *Rising* (Four Way Books, 2009) and the chapbook *Parents* (Immaculate Disciples Press, 2011). Her poems and essays have appeared in many publications including *The Awl, Drunken Boat, Harp & Altar, La Petite Zine, Lit, Ploughshares, Sixth Finch,* and *Typo.* Two of her poems were selected by Kevin Young for *The Best American Poetry 2011.* She lives in Brooklyn where she co-hosts an event series called Yardmeter Editions. She occasionally blogs at adultish.blogspot.com and is co-owner of Berl's Brooklyn Poetry Shop.